THE ESSENE GOSPEL OF PEACE

Book Two

THE UNKNOWN BOOKS OF THE ESSENES

Oh, the Ancient Truth!
Ages upon ages past it was found,
And it bound together a Noble Brotherhood.
The Ancient Truth!
Hold fast to it!

—Goethe

THE ESSENE GOSPEL OF PEACE

BOOK TWO

THE UNKNOWN BOOKS
OF THE ESSENES

*The Original Hebrew and Aramaic Texts
translated and edited by*

EDMOND BORDEAUX SZEKELY

MCMLXXXI
INTERNATIONAL BIOGENIC SOCIETY

SOME BOOKS BY EDMOND BORDEAUX SZEKELY

THE ESSENE WAY—BIOGENIC LIVING
THE ESSENE GOSPEL OF PEACE, BOOK ONE
BOOK TWO, THE UNKNOWN BOOKS OF THE ESSENES
BOOK THREE, LOST SCROLLS OF THE ESSENE BROTHERHOOD
BOOK FOUR, THE TEACHINGS OF THE ELECT
THE DISCOVERY OF THE ESSENE GOSPEL: The Essenes & the Vatican
SEARCH FOR THE AGELESS, in Three Volumes
THE ESSENE BOOK OF CREATION
THE ESSENE JESUS
THE ESSENE BOOK OF ASHA
THE ZEND AVESTA OF ZARATHUSTRA
ARCHEOSOPHY, A NEW SCIENCE
THE ESSENE ORIGINS OF CHRISTIANITY
TEACHINGS OF THE ESSENES FROM ENOCH TO THE DEAD SEA SCROLLS
THE ESSENES, BY JOSEPHUS AND HIS CONTEMPORARIES
THE ESSENE TEACHINGS OF ZARATHUSTRA
THE ESSENE SCIENCE OF LIFE
THE ESSENE CODE OF LIFE
THE ESSENE SCIENCE OF FASTING AND THE ART OF SOBRIETY
ESSENE COMMUNIONS WITH THE INFINITE
THE FIRST ESSENE
THE BIOGENIC REVOLUTION
THE ORIGIN OF LIFE
THE COSMOTHERAPY OF THE ESSENES
THE LIVING BUDDHA
MAN IN THE COSMIC OCEAN
TOWARD THE CONQUEST OF THE INNER COSMOS
FATHER, GIVE US ANOTHER CHANCE
THE ECOLOGICAL HEALTH GARDEN, THE BOOK OF SURVIVAL
THE TENDER TOUCH: BIOGENIC FULFILLMENT
THE DIALECTICAL METHOD OF THINKING
THE EVOLUTION OF HUMAN THOUGHT
THE SOUL OF ANCIENT MEXICO
THE NEW FIRE
ANCIENT AMERICA: PARADISE LOST
DEATH OF THE NEW WORLD
PILGRIM OF THE HIMALAYAS
MESSENGERS FROM ANCIENT CIVILIZATIONS
SEXUAL HARMONY and Raising Happy, Healthy Children
LUDWIG VAN BEETHOVEN, PROMETHEUS OF THE MODERN WORLD
THE FIERY CHARIOTS
CREATIVE WORK: KARMA YOGA
THE ART OF STUDY: THE SORBONNE METHOD
COSMOS, MAN AND SOCIETY
THE BOOK OF LIVING FOODS
SCIENTIFIC VEGETARIANISM
THE CONQUEST OF DEATH

Book Design by Golondrina Graphics

This Book Two
of the Essene Gospel of Peace
is dedicated to all those
who have waited patiently for forty years
in the spiritual desert of the twentieth century
for the promised land,
the continuation of Book One,
disseminated in 200,000 copies
in seventeen languages. *

E.B.S.

*At the time of this printing, Book One has been disseminated
in more than a million copies in twenty-six languages.

CONTENTS

PREFACE

Book Two of the Essene Gospel of Peace

I have to begin this preface with a great confession: this is not my first translation of Book Two of the Essene Gospel of Peace; it is my second. The first effort took many years to complete, and it was composed painstakingly and literally, with hundreds of cross references and abundant philological and exegetical footnotes. When it was finished, I was very proud of it, and in a glow of self-satisfied accomplishment, I gave it to my friend, Aldous Huxley, to read. Two weeks later, I asked him what he thought of my monumental translation. "It is very, very bad," he answered. "It is even worse than the most boring treatises of the patristics and scholastics, which nobody reads today. It is so dry and uninteresting, in fact, that I have no desire to read Book Three." I was speechless, so he continued. "You should rewrite it, and give it some of the vitality of your other books—make it literary, readable and attractive for twentieth century readers. I'm sure the Essenes did not speak to each other in footnotes! In the form it is in now, the only readers you will have for it may be a few dogmatists in theological seminaries, who seem to take masochistic pleasure in reading this sort of thing. However," he added with a smile, "you might find some value in it as a cure for insomnia; each time I tried to read it I fell asleep in a few minutes. You might try to sell a few copies that way by advertising a new sleep remedy in the health magazines—no harmful chemicals, and all that."

It took me a long time to recuperate from his criticism. I put aside the manuscript for years. Meanwhile, I continued to receive thousands of letters from many readers from all parts of the world of my translation of Book One of the Essene Gospel of Peace, asking for the second and third books promised in the preface. Finally, I got the courage to start again. The passing of the years had mellowed my attitude and I saw my friend's criticism in a new light. I rewrote the entire manuscript, treating it as literature and poetry, coming to grips with the great problems of life, both ancient and contemporary. It was not easy to be faithful to the original, and at the same time to present the eternal truths in a way that would appeal to twentieth century man. And yet, it was vitally important that I try; for the Essenes, above all others, strove to win the hearts of men through reason, and the powerful and vivid example of their lives.

Sadly, Aldous is no longer here to read my second translation. I have a feeling he would have liked it (not a single footnote!), but I will have to leave the final judgment to my readers. If Books Two and Three will become as popular as Book One, my efforts of many, many years will be amply rewarded.

EDMOND BORDEAUX SZEKELY

San Diego, California
the first of November, 1974.

INTRODUCTION

There are three paths leading to Truth. The first is the path of the consciousness, the second that of nature, and the third is the accumulated experience of past generations, which we receive in the shape of the great masterpieces of all ages. From time immemorial, man and humanity have followed all three paths.

The first path to Truth, the path of the consciousness, is that followed by the great mystics. They consider that the consciousness is the most immediate reality for us and is the key to the universe. It is something which is in us, which *is* us. And throughout the ages the mystics have made the discovery that the laws of human consciousness contain an aspect not found in the laws governing the material universe.

A certain dynamic unity exists in our consciousness, where one is at the same time many. It is possible for us to have simultaneously different thoughts, ideas, associations, images, memories and intuitions occupying our consciousness within fragments of a minute or a second, yet all this multiplicity will still constitute only a single dynamic unity. Therefore the laws of mathematics, which are valid for the material universe and are a key to its understanding, will not be valid in the field of consciousness, a realm where two and two do not necessarily make four. The mystics also found that measurements of space, time and weight, universally valid in nature and throughout the material universe, are not applicable to the consciousness, where sometimes a few seconds seem like hours, or hours like a minute.

Our consciousness does not exist in space and therefore cannot be measured in spatial terms. It has its own time, which is very often timelessness, so temporal measurements cannot be applied to Truth reached by this path. The great mystics discovered that the human consciousness, besides being the most immediate and the inmost reality for us, is at the same time our closest source of energy, harmony and knowledge. The path to Truth leading to and through the consciousness produced the great teachings of humanity, the great intuitions and the great masterpieces throughout the ages. Such then is the first path to or source of Truth, as the Essene traditions understand and interpret it.

Unfortunately, the magnificent original intuitions of the great masters often lose their vitality as they pass down the generations. They are very often modified, distorted and turned into dogmas, and all too frequently their values become petrified in institutions and organized hierarchies. The pure intuitions are choked by the sands of time, and eventually have to be dug out by seekers of Truth able to penetrate into their essence.

Another danger is that persons following this path to Truth—the path of the consciousness—may fall into exaggerations. They come to think that this is the only path to Truth and disregard all others. Very often, too, they apply the specific laws of the human consciousness to the material universe where they lack validity, and ignore the laws proper to the latter sphere. The mystic often creates for himself an artificial universe, farther and farther removed from reality, till he ends by living in an ivory tower, having lost all contact with reality and life.

The second of the three paths is the path of nature. While the first path of the consciousness starts from within and penetrates thence into the totality of things, the second path takes the opposite way. Its starting point is the external world. It is the path of the scientist, and has been followed in all ages through experience and through experiment, through the use of inductive and deductive methods. The scientist, working with exact quantitative measurements, measures everything in space and time, and makes all possible correlations.

With his telescope he penetrates into far-distant cosmic space, into the various solar and galactic systems; through spectrum analysis he measures the constituents of the different planets in cosmic space; and by mathematical calculation he establishes in advance the movements of celestial bodies. Applying the law of cause and effect, the scientist establishes a long chain of causes and effects which help him to explain and measure the universe, as well as life.

But the scientist, like the mystic, sometimes falls into exaggerations. While science has transformed the life of mankind and has created great values for man in all ages, it has failed to give entire satisfaction in the solution of the final problems of existence, life and the universe. The scientist has the long chain of causes and effects secure in all its particles, but he has no idea what to do with the end of the chain. He has no solid point to which he may attach the end of the chain, and so by the path to Truth through nature and the material universe he is unable to answer the great and eternal questions concerning the beginning and end of all things.

The greatest scientists recognize that in the metaphysical field beyond the scientific chain there is something else—continuing from the end of that chain. However, there are also the dogmatic scientists who deny any other approach to Truth than their own, who refuse to attribute reality to the facts and phenomena which they cannot fit neatly into their own categories and classifications.

The path to Truth through nature is not that of the dogmatic scientist, just as the first path is not that of the one-sided mystic. Nature is a great open book in which everything can be found, if we learn to draw from it the inspiration which it has given to the great thinkers of all ages. If we learn her language, nature will reveal to us all the laws of life and the universe.

It is for this reason that all the great masters of humanity from time to time withdrew into nature: Zarathustra and Moses into the mountains, Buddha to the forest, Jesus and the Essenes to the desert—and thus followed this second path as well as that of the consciousness. The two paths do not contradict one another, but harmoniously complete one another in full knowledge of the laws of both. It was thus that the great teachers reached wonderful and deeply profound truths which have given inspiration to millions through thousands of years.

The third path to Truth, is the wisdom, knowledge and experience acquired by the great thinkers of all ages and transmitted to us in the form of great teachings, the great sacred books or scriptures, and the great masterpieces of universal literature which together form what today we would call universal culture. In brief, therefore, our approach to Truth is a threefold one: through consciousness, nature and culture.

In the following chapters we shall follow this threefold path leading to Truth and shall examine and translate some of the great sacred writings of the Essenes.

There are different ways of studying these great writings. One way—the way of all theologians and of the organized Churches—is to consider each text literally. This is the dogmatic way resulting from a long process of petrification, by which truths are inevitably transformed into dogmas.

When the theologian follows this most easy but one-sided path, he runs into endless contradictions and complications, and he reaches a conclusion as far removed from the truth as that of the scientific interpreter of these texts who rejects them as entirely valueless and without validity. The approaches of the dogmatic theologian and the exclusivist scientist represent two extremes.

A third error is to believe, as do certain symbolists, that these books have no more than a symbolic content and are nothing more than parables. With their own particular way of exaggeration these symbolists make thousands of different and quite contradictory interpretations of these great texts. The spirit of the Essene traditions is opposed to all three of these ways of interpreting these ageless writings and follows an entirely different approach.

The Essene method of interpretation of these books is, on the one hand, to place them in harmonious correlation with the laws of the human consciousness and of nature, and, on the other, to consider the facts and circumstances of the age and environment in which they were written. This approach also takes into account the degree of evolution and understanding of the people to whom the particular master was addressing his message.

Since all the great masters had to adapt their teaching to the level of their audience, they found it necessary to formulate both an exoteric and esoteric teaching. The exoteric message was one comprehensible to the people at large and was expressed in terms of various rules, forms and rituals corresponding to the basic needs of the people and the age concerned. Parallel with this, the esoteric teachings have survived through the ages partly as written and partly as unwritten living traditions, free from forms, rituals, rules and dogmas, and in all periods have been kept alive and practised by a small minority.

It is in this spirit of the interpretation of the Truth that the Essene Gospel of Peace will be translated in the following pages. Rejecting the dogmatic methods of literal and purely scientific interpretation as well as the exaggeration of the symbolists, we shall try to translate the Essene Gospel of Peace in the light of our consciousness and of nature, and in harmony with the great traditions of the Essenes, to whose brotherhood the authors of the Dead Sea Scrolls themselves belonged.

THE VISION OF ENOCH

THE MOST ANCIENT REVELATION

God Speaks to Man

I speak to you.
Be still
Know
I am
God.

I spoke to you
When you were born.
Be still
Know
I am
God.

I spoke to you
At your first sight.
Be still
Know
I am
God.

I spoke to you
At your first word.
Be still
Know
I am
God.

I spoke to you
At your first thought.
Be still
Know
I am
God.

I spoke to you
At your first love.
Be still
Know
I am
God.

I spoke to you
At your first song.
Be still
Know
I am
God.

I speak to you
Through the grass of the meadows.
Be still
Know
I am
God.

I speak to you
Through the trees of the forests.
Be still
Know

I am
God.

I speak to you
Through the valleys and the hills.
Be still
Know
I am
God.

I speak to you
Through the Holy Mountains.
Be still
Know
I am
God.

I speak to you
Through the rain and the snow.
Be still
Know
I am
God.

I speak to you
Through the waves of the sea.
Be still
Know
I am
God.

I speak to you

Through the dew of the morning.
Be still
Know
I am
God.

I speak to you
Through the peace of the evening.
Be still
Know
I am
God.

I speak to you
Through the splendor of the sun.
Be still
Know
I am
God.

I speak to you
Through the brilliant stars.
Be still
Know
I am
God.

I speak to you
Through the storm and the clouds.
Be still
Know
I am

God.

I speak to you
Through the thunder and lightning.
Be still
Know
I am
God.

I speak to you
Through the mysterious rainbow.
Be still
Know
I am
God.

I will speak to you
When you are alone.
Be still
Know
I am
God.

I will speak to you
Through the Wisdom of the Ancients.
Be still
Know
I am
God.

I will speak to you
At the end of time.

Be still
Know
I am
God.

I will speak to you
When you have seen my Angels.
Be still
Know
I am
God.

I will speak to you
Throughout Eternity.
Be still
Know
I am
God.

I speak to you.
Be still
Know
I am
God.

FROM THE ESSENE BOOK OF MOSES

THE TEN COMMANDMENTS

And Mount Sinai was altogether in smoke because the Lord descended upon it in fire: and the smoke thereof ascended as the smoke of a furnace, and the whole mount quaked greatly.

And the Lord came down upon Mount Sinai, on the top of the mount: and the Lord called Moses up to the top of the mount: and Moses went up.

And the Lord called unto Moses out of the mountain, saying, Come unto me, for I would give thee the Law for thy people, which shall be a covenant for the Children of Light.

And Moses went up unto God. And God spake all these words, saying,

I am the Law, thy God, which hath brought thee out from the depths of the bondage of darkness.

Thou shalt have no other Laws before me.

Thou shalt not make unto thee any image of the Law in heaven above or in the earth beneath. I am the invisible Law, without beginning and without end.

Thou shalt not make unto thee false laws, for I am the Law, and the whole Law of all laws. If thou forsake me, thou shalt be visited by disasters for generation upon generation.

If thou keepest my commandments, thou shalt enter the In-finite Garden where stands the Tree of Life in the midst of the Eternal Sea.

Thou shalt not violate the Law. The Law is thy God, who shall not hold thee guiltless.

Honor thy Earthly Mother, that thy days may be long upon the land, and honor thy Heavenly Father, that eternal life be thine in the heavens, for the earth and the heavens are given unto thee by the Law, which is thy God.

Thou shalt greet thy Earthly Mother on the morning of the Sabbath.

Thou shalt greet the Angel of Earth on the second morning.

Thou shalt greet the Angel of Life on the third morning.

Thou shalt greet the Angel of Joy on the fourth morning.
Thou shalt greet the Angel of Sun on the fifth morning.
Thou shalt greet the Angel of Water on the sixth morning.
Thou shalt greet the Angel of Air on the seventh morning.
All these Angels of the Earthly Mother shalt thou greet, and consecrate thyself to them, that thou mayest enter the Infinite Garden where stands the Tree of Life.

Thou shalt worship thy Heavenly Father on the evening of the Sabbath.

Thou shalt commune with the Angel of Eternal Life on the second evening.

Thou shalt commune with the Angel of Work on the third evening.

Thou shalt commune with the Angel of Peace on the fourth evening.

Thou shalt commune with the Angel of Power on the fifth evening.

Thou shalt commune with the Angel of Love on the sixth evening.

Thou shalt commune with the Angel of Wisdom on the seventh evening.

All these Angels of the Heavenly Father shalt thou commune with, that thy soul may bathe in the Fountain of Light, and enter into the Sea of Eternity.

The seventh day is the Sabbath: thou shalt remember it, and keep it holy. The Sabbath is the day of the Light of the Law, thy God. In it thou shalt not do any work, but search the Light, the Kingdom of thy God, and all things shall be given unto thee.

For know ye that during six days thou shalt work with the Angels, but the seventh day shalt thou dwell in the Light of thy Lord, who is the holy Law.

Thou shalt not take the life from any living thing. Life comes only from God, who giveth it and taketh it away.

Thou shalt not debase Love. It is the sacred gift of thy Heavenly Father.

Thou shalt not trade thy Soul, the priceless gift of the loving

God, for the riches of the world, which are as seeds sown on stony ground, having no root in themselves, and so enduring but for a little while.

Thou shalt not be a false witness of the Law, to use it against thy brother: Only God knoweth the beginning and the ending of all things, for his eye is single, and he is the holy Law.

Thou shalt not covet thy neighbor's possessions. The Law giveth unto thee much greater gifts, even the earth and the heavens, if thou keep the Commandments of the Lord thy God.

And Moses heard the voice of the Lord, and sealed within him the covenant that was between the Lord and the Children of Light.

And Moses turned, and went down from the mount, and the two tablets of the Law were in his hand.

And the tablets were the work of God, and the writing was the writing of God, graven upon the tablets.

And the people knew not what became of Moses, and they gathered themselves together and brake off their golden earrings and made a molten calf. And they worshipped unto the idol, and offered to it burnt offerings.

And they ate and drank and danced before the golden calf, which they had made, and they abandoned themselves to corruption and evil before the Lord.

And it came to pass, as soon as he came nigh unto the camp, that he saw the calf, and the dancing, and the wickedness of the people: and Moses' anger waxed hot, and he cast the tablets out of his hands, and brake them beneath the mount.

And it came to pass on the morrow, that Moses said unto the people, Ye have sinned a great sin, ye have denied thy Creator. I will go up unto the Lord and plead atonement for thy sin.

And Moses returned unto the Lord, and said, Lord, thou hast seen the desecration of thy Holy Law. For thy children lost faith, and worshipped the darkness, and made for themselves a golden calf. Lord, forgive them, for they are blind to the light.

And the Lord said unto Moses, Behold, at the beginning of time was a covenant made between God and man, and the holy flame of the Creator did enter unto him. And he was made the son of

God, and it was given him to guard his inheritance of the first-born, and to make fruitful the land of his Father and keep it holy. And he who casteth out the Creator from him doth spit upon his birthright, and no more grievous sin doth exist in the eyes of God.

And the Lord spoke, saying, *Only the Children of Light can keep the Commandments of the Law. Hear me, for I say thus: the tablets which thou didst break, these shall nevermore be written in the words of men. As thou didst return them to the earth and fire, so shall they live, invisible, in the hearts of those who are able to follow their Law. To thy people of little faith, who did sin against the Creator, even whilst thou stood on holy ground before thy God, I will give another Law. It shall be a stern law, yea, it shall bind them, for they know not yet the Kingdom of Light.*

And Moses hid the invisible Law within his breast, and kept it for a sign to the Children of Light. And God gave unto Moses the written law for the people, and he went down unto them, and spake unto them with a heavy heart.

And Moses said unto the people, these are the laws which thy God hath given thee.

Thou shalt have no other gods before me.

Thou shalt not make unto thee any graven image.

Thou shalt not take the name of the Lord thy God in vain.

Remember the Sabbath day, to keep it holy.

Honor thy father and thy mother.

Thou shalt not kill.

Thou shalt not commit adultery.

Thou shalt not steal.

Thou shalt not bear false witness against thy neighbor.

Thou shalt not covet thy neighbor's house, nor thy neighbor's wife, nor anything that is thy neighbor's.

And there was a day of mourning and atonement for the great sin against the Creator, which did not end. And the broken tablets of the Invisible Law lived hidden in the breast of Moses, until it came to pass that the Children of Light appeared in the desert, and the angels walked the earth.

And it was by the bed of a stream, that the weary and afflicted came again to seek out Jesus. And like children, they had forgotten the Law; and like children, they sought out their father to show them where they had erred, and to set their feet again upon the path. And when the sun rose over the earth's rim they saw Jesus coming toward them from the mountain, with the brightness of the rising sun about his head.

And he raised his hand and smiled upon them, saying, "Peace be with you."

But they were ashamed to return his greeting, for each in his own way had turned his back on the holy teachings, and the Angels of the Earthly Mother and the Heavenly Father were not with them. And one man looked up in anguish and spoke: "Master, we are in sore need of your wisdom. For we know that which is good, and yet we follow evil. We know that to enter the kingdom of heaven we must walk with the angels of the day and of the night, yet our feet walk in the ways of the wicked. The light of day shines only on our pursuit of pleasure, and the night falls on our heedless stupor. Tell us, Master, how may we talk with the angels, and stay within their holy circle, that the Law may burn in our hearts with a constant flame?"

And Jesus spoke to them:

"To lift your eyes to heaven
When all mens' eyes are on the ground,
Is not easy.
To worship at the feet of the angels
When all men worship only fame and riches,
Is not easy.
But the most difficult of all
Is to think the thoughts of the angels,
To speak the words of the angels,
And to do as angels do."

And one man spoke: "But, Master, we are but men, we are not angels. How then can we hope to walk in their ways? Tell us what we must do."

And Jesus spoke:

> "As the son inherits the land of his father,
> So have we inherited a Holy Land
> From our Fathers.
> This land is not a field to be ploughed,
> But a place within us
> Where we may build our Holy Temple.
> And even as a temple must be raised,
> Stone by stone,
> So will I give to you those stones
> For the building of the Holy Temple;
> That which we have inherited
> From our Fathers,
> And their Fathers' Fathers."

And all the men gathered around Jesus, and their faces shone with desire to hear the words which would come from his lips. And he lifted his face to the rising sun, and the radiance of its rays filled his eyes as he spoke:

> "The Holy Temple can be built
> Only with the ancient Communions,
> Those which are spoken,
> Those which are thought,
> And those which are lived.
> For if they are spoken only with the mouth,
> They are as a dead hive
> Which the bees have forsaken,
> That gives no more honey.
> The Communions are a bridge
> Between man and the angels,

And like a bridge,
Can be built only with patience,
Yea, even as the bridge over the river
Is fashioned stone by stone,
As they are found by the water's edge.

And the Communions are fourteen in number,
As the Angels of the Heavenly Father
Number seven,
And the Angels of the Earthly Mother
Number seven.
And just as the roots of the tree
Sink into the earth and are nourished,
And the branches of the tree
Raise their arms to heaven,
So is man like the trunk of the tree,
With his roots deep
In the breast of his Earthly Mother,
And his soul ascending
To the bright stars of his Heavenly Father.
And the roots of the tree
Are the Angels of the Earthly Mother,
And the branches of the tree
Are the Angels of the Heavenly Father.
And this is the sacred Tree of Life
Which stands in the Sea of Eternity.

The first Communion is with
The Angel of Sun,
She who cometh each morning
As a bride from her chamber,
To shed her golden light on the world.
O thou immortal, shining, swift-steeded

Angel of the Sun!
There is no warmth without thee,
No fire without thee,
No life without thee.
The green leaves of the trees
Do worship thee,
And through thee is the tiny wheat kernel
Become a river of golden grass,
Moving with the wind.
Through thee is opened the flower
In the center of my body.
Therefore will I never hide myself
From thee.
Angel of Sun,
Holy messenger of the Earthly Mother,
Enter the holy temple within me
And give me the Fire of Life!

The second Communion is with
The Angel of Water,
She who makes the rain
To fall on the arid plain,
Who fills the dry well to overflowing.
Yea, we do worship thee,
Water of Life.
From the heavenly sea
The waters run and flow forward
From the never-failing springs.
In my blood flow
A thousand pure springs,
And vapors, and clouds,
And all the waters

That spread over all the seven Kingdoms.
All the waters
The Creator hath made
Are holy.
The voice of the Lord
Is upon the waters:
The God of Glory thundereth;
The Lord is upon many waters.
Angel of Water,
Holy messenger of the Earthly Mother,
Enter the blood that flows through me,
Wash my body in the rain
That falls from heaven,
And give me the Water of Life!

The third Communion is with
The Angel of Air,
Who spreads the perfume
Of sweet-smelling fields,
Of spring grass after rain,
Of the opening buds of the
Rose of Sharon.
We worship the Holy Breath
Which is placed higher
Than all the other things created.
For, lo, the eternal and sovereign
Luminous space,
Where rule the unnumbered stars,
Is the air we breathe in
And the air we breathe out.
And in the moment betwixt the breathing in
And the breathing out

Is hidden all the mysteries
Of the Infinite Garden.
Angel of Air,
Holy messenger of the Earthly Mother,
Enter deep within me,
As the swallow plummets from the sky,
That I may know the secrets of the wind
And the music of the stars.

The fourth Communion is with
The Angel of Earth,
She who brings forth corn and grapes
From the fulness of the earth,
She who brings children
From the loins of husband and wife.
He who would till the earth,
With the left arm and the right,
Unto him will she bring forth
An abundance of fruit and grain,
Golden-hued plants
Growing up from the earth
During the spring,
As far as the earth extends,
As far as the rivers stretch,
As far as the sun rises,
To impart their gifts of food unto men.
This wide earth do I praise,
Expanded far with paths,
The productive, the full-bearing,
Thy Mother, holy plant!
Yea, I praise the lands
Where thou dost grow,

Sweet-scented, swiftly spreading,
The good growth of the Lord.
He who sows corn, grass and fruit,
Soweth the Law.
And his harvest shall be bountiful,
And his crop shall be ripe upon the hills.
As a reward for the followers of the Law,
The Lord sent the Angel of Earth,
Holy messenger of the Earthly Mother,
To make the plants to grow,
And to make fertile the womb of woman,
That the earth may never be without
The laughter of children.
Let us worship the Lord in her!

The fifth Communion is with
The Angel of Life,
She who gives strength and vigor to man.
For, lo, if the wax is not pure,
How then can the candle give a steady flame?
Go, then, toward the high-growing trees,
And before one of them which is beautiful,
High-growing and mighty,
Say these words:
'Hail be unto thee! O good, living tree,
Made by the Creator!'
Then shall the River of Life
Flow between you and your Brother,
The Tree,
And health of the body,
Swiftness of foot,
Quick hearing of the ears,

Strength of the arms
And eyesight of the eagle be yours.
Such is the Communion
With the Angel of Life,
Holy messenger of the Earthly Mother.

The sixth Communion is with
The Angel of Joy,
She who descends upon earth
To give beauty to all men.
For the Lord is not worshipped with sadness,
Nor with cries of despair.
Leave off your moans and lamentations,
And sing unto the Lord a new song:
Sing unto the Lord, all the earth.
Let the heavens rejoice
And let the earth be glad.
Let the field be joyful,
Let the floods clap their hands;
Let the hills be joyful together
Before the Lord.
For you shall go out with joy
And be led forth with peace:
The mountains and the hills
Shall break forth before you into singing.
Angel of Joy,
Holy messenger of the Earthly Mother,
I will sing unto the Lord
As long as I live:
I will sing praise to my God
While I have my being.

The seventh Communion is with
Our Earthly Mother,
She who sends forth her Angels
To guide the roots of man
And send them deep into the blessed soil.
We invoke the Earthly Mother!
The Holy Preserver!
The Maintainer!
It is She who will restore the world!
The earth is hers,
And the fulness thereof: the world,
And they that dwell therein.
We worship the good, the strong,
The beneficent Earthly Mother
And all her Angels,
Bounteous, valiant,
And full of strength;
Welfare-bestowing, kind,
And health-giving.
Through her brightness and glory
Do the plants grow up from the earth,
By the never-failing springs.
Through her brightness and glory
Do the winds blow,
Driving down the clouds
Towards the never-failing springs.
The Earthly Mother and I are One.
I have my roots in her,
And she takes her delight in me,
According to the Holy Law."

Then there was a great silence, as the listeners pondered the words of Jesus. And there was new strength in them, and desire and hope shone in their faces. And then one man spoke: "Master, we are filled with eagerness to begin our Communions with the Angels of the Earthly Mother, who planted the Great Garden of the Earth. But what of the Angels of the Heavenly Father, who rule the night? How are we to talk to them, who are so far above us, who are invisible to our eyes? For we can see the rays of the sun, we can feel the cool water of the stream where we bathe, and the grapes are warm to our touch as they grow purple on the vines. But the Angels of the Heavenly Father cannot be seen, or heard, or touched. How then can we talk to them, and enter their Infinite Garden? Master, tell us what we must do."

And the morning sun encircled his head with glory as Jesus looked upon them and spoke:

> *"My children, know you not that the Earth*
> *And all that dwells therein*
> *Is but a reflection of the*
> *Kingdom of the Heavenly Father?*
> *And as you are suckled and comforted*
> *By your mother when a child,*
> *But go to join your father in the fields*
> *When you grow up,*
> *So do the Angels of the Earthly Mother*
> *Guide your steps*
> *Toward him who is your Father,*
> *And all his holy Angels,*
> *That you may know your true home*
> *And become true Sons of God.*
> *While we are children,*
> *We will see the rays of the sun,*
> *But not the Power which created it;*
> *While we are children,*
> *We will hear the sounds of the flowing brook,*
> *But not the Love which created it;*

While we are children,
We will see the stars,
But not the hand which scatters them
Through the sky,
As the farmer scatters his seed.
Only through the Communions
With the Angels of the Heavenly Father,
Will we learn to see the unseen,
To hear that which cannot be heard,
And to speak the unspoken word.

The first Communion is with
The Angel of Power,
Who fills the sun with heat,
And guides the hand of man
In all his works.
Thine, O Heavenly Father!
Was the Power,
When thou didst order a path
For each of us and all.
Through thy power
Will my feet tread the
Path of the Law;
Through thy power
Will my hands perform thy works.
May the golden river of power
Always flow from thee to me,
And may my body always turn unto thee,
As the flower turns unto the sun.
For there is no power save that
From the Heavenly Father;
All else is but a dream of dust,

A cloud passing over the face of the sun.
There is no man that hath power
Over the spirit;
Neither hath he power in the day of death.
Only that power which cometh from God
Can carry us out from the City of Death.
Guide our works and deeds,
O Angel of Power,
Holy messenger of the Heavenly Father!

The second Communion is with
The Angel of Love,
Whose healing waters flow
In a never-ending stream
From the Sea of Eternity.
Beloved, let us love one another:
For love is of the Heavenly Father,
And every one that loveth
Is born of the Heavenly Order
And knoweth the Angels.
For without love,
A man's heart is parched and cracked
As the bottom of a dry well,
And his words are empty
As a hollow gourd.
But loving words are as a honeycomb
Sweet to the soul;
Loving words in a man's mouth
Are as deep waters,
And the wellspring of love
As a flowing brook.
Yea, it was said in the ancient of days,

Thou shalt love thy Heavenly Father
With all thy heart,
And with all thy mind,
And with all thy deeds,
And thou shalt love thy brothers
As thyself.
The Heavenly Father is love;
And he that dwelleth in love
Dwelleth in the Heavenly Father,
And the Heavenly Father in him.
He that loveth not is as a wandering bird
Cast out of the nest;
For him the grass faileth
And the stream has a bitter taste.
And if a man say,
I love the Heavenly Father
But hate my brother,
He is a liar:
For he that loveth not his brother
Whom he hath seen,
How can he love the Heavenly Father
Whom he hath not seen?
By this we know the Children of Light:
Those who walk with the Angel of Love,
For they love the Heavenly Father,
And they love their brethren,
And they keep the Holy Law.
Love is stronger
Than the currents of deep waters:
Love is stronger than death.

The third Communion is with

The Angel of Wisdom,
Who maketh man free from fear,
Wide of heart,
And easy of conscience:
Holy Wisdom,
The Understanding that unfolds,
Continuously,
As a holy scroll,
Yet does not come through learning.
All wisdom cometh
From the Heavenly Father,
And is with him for ever.
Who can number the sand of the sea,
And the drops of rain,
And the days of eternity?
Who can find out the height of heaven,
And the breadth of the earth?
Who can tell the beginning
Of wisdom?
Wisdom hath been created
Before all things.
He who is without wisdom
Is like unto him that saith to the wood,
'Awake', and to the dumb stone,
'Arise, and teach!'
So are his words empty,
And his deeds harmful,
As a child who brandishes his father's sword
And knoweth not its cutting edge.
But the crown of wisdom
Makes peace and perfect health
To flourish,

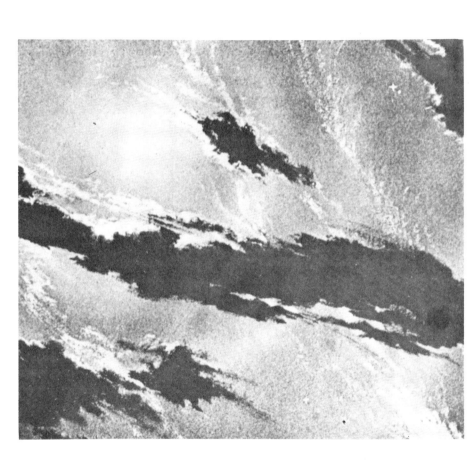

Both of which are the gifts of God.
O thou Heavenly Order!
And thou, Angel of Wisdom!
I will worship thee and
The Heavenly Father,
Because of whom
The river of thought within us
Is flowing towards the
Holy Sea of Eternity.

The fourth Communion is with
The Angel of Eternal Life,
Who brings the message of eternity
To man.
For he who walks with the Angels
Shall learn to soar
Above the clouds,
And his home shall be
In the Eternal Sea
Where stands the sacred Tree of Life.
Do not wait for death
To reveal the great mystery;
If you know not your Heavenly Father
While your feet tread the dusty soil,
There shall be naught but shadows for thee
In the life that is to come.
Here and now
Is the mystery revealed.
Here and now
Is the curtain lifted.
Be not afraid, O man!
Lay hold of the wings of the

Angel of Eternal Life,
And soar into the paths of the stars,
The moon, the sun,
And the endless Light,
Moving around in their
Revolving circle forever,
And fly toward the Heavenly Sea
Of Eternal Life.

The fifth Communion is with
The Angel of Work,
Who sings in the humming of the bee,
Pausing not in its making of golden honey;
In the flute of the shepherd,
Who sleeps not lest his flock go astray;
In the song of the maiden
As she lays her hand to the spindle.
And if you think that these
Are not as fair in the eyes of the Lord
As the loftiest of prayers
Echoed from the highest mountain,
Then you do indeed err.
For the honest work of humble hands
Is a daily prayer of thanksgiving,
And the music of the plough
Is a joyful song unto the Lord.
He who eats the bread of idleness
Must die of hunger,
For a field of stones
Can yield only stones.
For him is the day without meaning,
And the night a bitter journey of evil dreams.

The mind of the idle
Is full of the weeds of discontent;
But he who walks with the
Angel of Work
Has within him a field always fertile,
Where corn and grapes
And all manner of sweet-scented
Herbs and flowers grow in abundance.
As ye sow, so shall ye reap.
The man of God who has found his task
Shall not ask any other blessing.

The sixth Communion is with
The Angel of Peace,
Whose kiss bestoweth calm,
And whose face is as the surface
Of untroubled waters,
Wherein the moon is reflected.
I will invoke Peace,
Whose breath is friendly,
Whose hand smooths the troubled brow.
In the reign of Peace,
There is neither hunger nor thirst,
Neither cold wind nor hot wind,
Neither old age nor death.
But to him that hath not peace in his soul,
There is no place to build within
The Holy Temple;
For how can the carpenter build
In the midst of a whirlwind?
The seed of violence can reap
Only a harvest of desolation,

And from the parched clay
Can grow no living thing.
Seek ye then the Angel of Peace,
Who is as the morning star
In the midst of a cloud,
As the moon at the full,
As a fair olive tree budding forth fruit,
And as the sun shining on the temple
Of the most High.
Peace dwells in the heart of silence:
Be still, and know that I am God.

The seventh Communion is with
The Heavenly Father,
Who is,
Who was, and
Who ever shall be.
O Great Creator!
Thou didst create the Heavenly Angels,
And thou didst reveal the
Heavenly Laws!
Thou art my refuge and my fortress,
Thou art from everlasting.
Lord, thou hast been our dwelling place
In all generations.
Before the mountains were brought forth,
Or ever thou hadst formed the earth,
Even from everlasting to everlasting,
Thou art God.
Who hath made the waters,
And who maketh the plants?
Who to the wind

Hath yoked the storm-clouds,
The swift and even the fleetest?
Who, O Great Creator!
Is the fountain of Eternal Life
Within our souls?
Who hath made the Light and the Darkness?
Who hath made sleep
And the zest of the waking hours?
Who spread the noontides
And the midnight?
Thou, O Great Creator!
Thou hast made the earth
By thy power,
Hath established the world
By thy wisdom,
And hath stretched out the heavens
By thy love.
Do thou reveal unto me,
O Heavenly Father,
Thy nature,
Which is the power of the
Angels of thy Holy Kingdom.
Immortality and the Heavenly Order
Hast thou given, O Creator,
And the best of all things,
Thy Holy Law!
I will praise thy works
With songs of thanksgiving,
Continually,
In all the generations of time.
With the coming of day
I embrace my Mother,

With the coming of night,
I join my Father,
And with the outgoing
Of evening and morning
I will breathe Their Law,
And I will not interrupt these Communions
Until the end of time."

And over heaven and earth was a great silence, and the peace of the Heavenly Father and the Earthly Mother shone over the heads of Jesus and the multitude.

THE SEVENFOLD PEACE

And seeing the multitudes, Jesus went up into a mountain, and his disciples came unto him, and all those who hungered for his words. And seeing them gathered, he opened his mouth and taught them, saying:

"Peace I bring to thee, my children,
The Sevenfold Peace
Of the Earthly Mother
And the Heavenly Father.
Peace I bring to thy body,
Guided by the Angel of Power;
Peace I bring to thy heart,
Guided by the Angel of Love;
Peace I bring to thy mind,
Guided by the Angel of Wisdom.
Through the Angels of
Power, Love and Wisdom,
Thou shalt travel the Seven Paths
Of the Infinite Garden,
And thy body, thy heart and thy mind
Shall join in Oneness
In the Sacred Flight to the
Heavenly Sea of Peace.

Yea, I tell thee truly,
The paths are seven
Through the Infinite Garden,
And each must be traversed
By the body, the heart and the mind
As one,
Lest thou stumble and fall

Into the abyss of emptiness.
For as a bird cannot fly with one wing,
So doth thy Bird of Wisdom
Need two wings of Power and Love
To soar above the abyss
To the Holy Tree of Life.

For the body alone
Is an abandoned house seen from afar:
What was thought beautiful
Is but ruin and desolation
When drawing near.
The body alone
Is as a chariot fashioned from gold,
Whose maker sets it on a pedestal,
Loath to soil it with use.
But as a golden idol,
It is ugly and without grace,
For only in movement
Doth it reveal its purpose.
Like the hollow blackness of a window
When the wind puts out its candle,
Is the body alone,
With no heart and no mind
To fill it with light.

And the heart alone
Is a sun with no earth to shine upon,
A light in the void,
A ball of warmth drowned
In a sea of blackness.
For when a man doth love,
That love turneth only to

Its own destruction
When there is no hand to stretch forth
In good works,
And no mind to weave the flames of desire
Into a tapestry of psalms.
Like a whirlwind in the desert
Is the heart alone,
With no body and no mind
To lead it singing
Through the cypress and the pine.

And the mind alone
Is a holy scroll
Which has worn thin with the years,
And must be buried.
The truth and beauty of its words
Have not changed,
But the eyes can no longer read
The faded letters,
And it falleth to pieces in the hands.
So is the mind without the heart
To give it words,
And without the body
To do its deeds.
For what availeth wisdom
Without a heart to feel
And a tongue to give it voice?
Barren as the womb of an aged woman
Is the mind alone,
With no heart and no body
To fill it with life.

For, lo, I tell thee truly,

The body and the heart and the mind
Are as a chariot, and a horse, and a driver.
The chariot is the body,
Forged in strength to do the will
Of the Heavenly Father
And the Earthly Mother.
The heart is the fiery steed,
Glorious and courageous,
Who carries the chariot bravely,
Whether the road be smooth,
Or whether stones and fallen trees
Lie in its path.
And the driver is the mind,
Holding the reins of wisdom,
Seeing from above what lieth
On the far horizon,
Charting the course of hoofs and wheels.

Give ear, O ye heavens,
And I will speak;
And hear, O earth,
The words of my mouth.
My doctrine shall drop as the rain,
My speech shall distil as the dew,
As the small rain
Upon the tender herb,
And as the showers upon the grass.

Blessed is the Child of Light
Who is strong in body,
For he shall have oneness with the earth.
Thou shalt celebrate a daily feast
With all the gifts of the Angel of Earth:

The golden wheat and corn,
The purple grapes of autumn,
The ripe fruits of the trees,
The amber honey of the bees.
Thou shalt seek the fresh air
Of the forest and of the fields,
And there in the midst of them
Shalt thou find the Angel of Air.
Put off thy shoes and clothing
And suffer the Angel of Air
To embrace all thy body.
Then shalt thou breathe long and deeply,
That the Angel of Air
May be brought within thee.
Enter into the cool and flowing river
And suffer the Angel of Water
To embrace all thy body.
Cast thyself wholly into his enfolding arms,
And as often as thou movest the air
With thy breath,
Move with thy body the water also.
Thou shalt seek the Angel of Sun,
And enter into that embrace
Which doth purify with holy flames.
And all these things are of the Holy Law
Of the Earthly Mother,
She who did give thee birth.
He who hath found peace with the body
Hath built a holy temple
Wherein may dwell forever
The spirit of God.
Know this peace with thy mind,

Desire this peace with thy heart,
Fulfill this peace with thy body.

Blessed is the Child of Light
Who is wise in mind,
For he shall create heaven.
The mind of the wise
Is a well-ploughed field,
Which giveth forth abundance and plenty.
For it thou showest a handful of seed
To a wise man,
He will see in his mind's eye
A field of golden wheat.
And if thou showest a handful of seed
To a fool,
He will see only that which is before him,
And call them worthless pebbles.
And as the field of the wise man
Giveth forth grain in abundance,
And the field of the fool
Is a harvest only of stones,
So it is with our thoughts.
As the sheaf of golden wheat
Lieth hidden within the tiny kernel,
So is the kingdom of heaven
Hidden within our thoughts.
If they be filled with the
Power, Love and Wisdom
Of the Angels of the Heavenly Father,
So they shall carry us
To the Heavenly Sea.
But if they be stained

With corruption, hatred and ignorance,
They shall chain our feet
To pillars of pain and suffering.
No man can serve two masters;
Neither can evil thoughts abide in a mind
Filled with the Light of the Law.
He who hath found peace with the mind
Hath learned to soar beyond
The Realm of the Angels.
Know this peace with thy mind,
Desire this peace with thy heart,
Fulfill this peace with thy body.

Blessed is the Child of Light
Who is pure in heart,
For he shall see God.
For as the Heavenly Father hath given thee
His holy spirit,
And thy Earthly Mother hath given thee
Her holy body,
So shall ye give love
To all thy brothers.
And thy true brothers are all those
Who do the will of thy Heavenly Father
And thy Earthly Mother.
Let thy love be as the sun
Which shines on all the creatures of the earth,
And does not favor one blade of grass
For another.
And this love shall flow as a fountain
From brother to brother,
And as it is spent,

So shall it be replenished.
For love is eternal.
Love is stronger
Than the currents of deep waters.
Love is stronger than death.
And if a man hath not love,
He doth build a wall between him
And all the creatures of the earth,
And therein doth he dwell
In loneliness and pain.
Or he may become as an angry whirlpool
Which sucks into its depths
All that floats too near.
For the heart is a sea with mighty waves,
And love and wisdom must temper it,
As the warm sun breaks through the clouds
And quiets the restless sea.
He who hath found peace with his brothers
Hath entered the kingdom of Love,
And shall see God face to face.
Know this peace with thy mind,
Desire this peace with thy heart,
Fulfill this peace with thy body.

Blessed is the Child of Light
Who doth build on earth
The kingdom of heaven,
For he shall dwell in both worlds.
Thou shalt follow the Law
Of the Brotherhood,
Which saith that none shall have wealth,
And none shall be poor,

And all shall work together
In the garden of the Brotherhood.
Yet each shall follow his own path,
And each shall commune with his own heart.
For in the Infinite Garden
There are many and diverse flowers:
Who shall say that one is best
Because its color is purple,
Or that one is favored
Because its stalk is long and slender?
Though the brothers
Be of different complexion,
Yet do they all toil
In the vineyard of the Earthly Mother,
And they all do lift their voices together
In praise of the Heavenly Father.
And together they break the holy bread,
And in silence share the holy meal
Of thanksgiving.
There shall be no peace among peoples
Till there be one garden of the brotherhood
Over the earth.
For how can there be peace
When each man pursueth his own gain
And doth sell his soul into slavery?
Thou, Child of Light,
Do ye gather with thy brothers
And then go ye forth
To teach the ways of the Law
To those who would hear.
He who hath found peace
With the brotherhood of man

Hath made himself
The co-worker of God.
Know this peace with thy mind,
Desire this peace with thy heart,
Fulfill this peace with thy body.

Blessed is the Child of Light
Who doth study the Book of the Law,
For he shall be as a candle
In the dark of night,
And an island of truth
In a sea of falsehood.
For know ye, that the written word
Which cometh from God
Is a reflection of the Heavenly Sea,
Even as the bright stars
Reflect the face of heaven.
As the words of the Ancient Ones
Are etched with the hand of God
On the Holy Scrolls,
So is the Law engraved on the hearts
Of the faithful who do study them.
For it was said of old,
That in the beginning there were giants
In the earth,
And mighty men which were of old,
Men of renown.
And the Children of Light
Shall guard and preserve
Their written word,
Lest we become again as beasts,
And know not the Kingdom of the Angels.

Know ye, too,
That only through the written word
Shalt thou find that Law
Which is unwritten,
As the spring which floweth from the ground
Hath a hidden source
In the secret depths beneath the earth.
The written Law
Is the instrument by which
The unwritten Law is understood,
As the mute branch of a tree
Becomes a singing flute
In the hands of the shepherd.
Many there are
Who would stay in the tranquil
Valley of ignorance,
Where children play
And butterflies dance in the sun
For their short hour of life.
But none can tarry there long,
And ahead rise the somber
Mountains of learning.
Many there are
Who fear to cross,
And many there are
Who have fallen bruised and bleeding
From their steep and rugged slopes.
But faith is the guide
Over the gaping chasm,
And perseverance the foothold
In the jagged rocks.
Beyond the icy peaks of struggle

Lies the peace and beauty
Of the Infinite Garden of Knowledge,
Where the meaning of the Law
Is made known to the Children of Light.
Here in the center of its forest
Stands the Tree of Life,
Mystery of mysteries.
He who hath found peace
With the teachings of the Ancients,
Through the light of the mind,
Through the light of nature,
And through the study of the Holy Word,
Hath entered the cloud-filled
Hall of the Ancients,
Where dwelleth the Holy Brotherhood,
Of whom no man may speak.
Know this peace with thy mind,
Desire this peace with thy heart,
Fulfill this peace with thy body.

Blessed is the Child of Light
Who knoweth his Earthly Mother,
For she is the giver of life.
Know that thy Mother is in thee,
And thou art in her.
She bore thee
And she giveth thee life.
She it was who gaveth thee thy body,
And to her shalt thou one day
Give it back again.
Know that the blood which runs in thee
Is born of the blood

Of thy Earthly Mother.
Her blood falls from the clouds,
Leaps up from the womb of the earth,
Babbles in the brooks of the mountains,
Flows wide in the rivers of the plains,
Sleeps in the lakes,
Rages mightily in the tempestuous seas.
Know that the air which thou dost breathe
Is born of the breath
Of thy Earthly Mother.
Her breath is azure
In the heights of the heavens,
Soughs in the tops of the mountains,
Whispers in the leaves of the forest,
Billows over the cornfields,
Slumbers in the deep valleys,
Burns hot in the desert.
Know that the hardness of thy bones
Is born of the bones
Of thy Earthly Mother,
Of the rocks and of the stones.
Know that the tenderness of thy flesh
Is born of the flesh
Of thy Earthly Mother,
She whose flesh waxeth yellow and red
In the fruits of the trees.
The light of thy eyes,
The hearing of thy ears,
These are born
Of the colors and the sounds
Of thy Earthly Mother,
Which doth enclose thee about,

As the waves of the sea enclose a fish,
As the eddying air a bird.
I tell thee in truth,
Man is the Son
Of the Earthly Mother,
And from her did the Son of Man
Receive his whole body,
Even as the body of the newborn babe
Is born of the womb of his mother.
I tell thee truly,
Thou art one with the Earthly Mother;
She is in thee, and thou art in her.
Of her wert thou born,
In her dost thou live,
And to her shalt thou return again.
Keep, therefore, her laws,
For none can live long,
Neither be happy,
But he who honors his Earthly Mother
And keepeth her laws.
For thy breath is her breath,
Thy blood her blood,
Thy bone her bone,
Thy flesh her flesh,
Thy eyes and thy ears
Are her eyes and her ears.
He who hath found peace
With his Earthly Mother
Shall never know death.
Know this peace with thy mind,
Desire this peace with thy heart,
Fulfill this peace with thy body.

Blessed is the Child of Light
Who doth seek his Heavenly Father,
For he shall have eternal life.
He that dwelleth in the secret place
Of the Most High
Shall abide under the shadow
Of the Almighty.
For he shall give his Angels charge over thee,
To keep thee in all thy ways.
Know ye that the Lord hath been
Our dwelling place
In all generations.
Before the mountains were brought forth,
Or ever he had formed
The earth and the world,
Even from everlasting to everlasting,
Hath there been love
Between the Heavenly Father
And his children.
And how shall this love be severed?
From the beginning
Until the ending of time
Doth the holy flame of love
Encircle the heads
Of the Heavenly Father
And the Children of Light:
How then shall this love be extinguished?
For not as a candle doth it burn,
Nor yet as a fire raging in the forest.
Lo, it burneth with the flame
Of Eternal Light,
And that flame cannot be consumed.

Ye that love thy Heavenly Father,
Do ye then his bidding:
Walk ye with his Holy Angels,
And find thy peace with his Holy Law.
For his Law is the entire Law:
Yea, it is the Law of laws.
Through his Law he hath made
The earth and the heavens to be one;
The mountains and the sea
Are his footstools.
With his hands he hath made us
And fashioned us,
And he gaveth us understanding
That we may learn his Law.
He is covered with Light
As with a garment:
He stretcheth out the heavens
Like a curtain.
He maketh the clouds his chariot;
He walketh upon the wings of the wind.
He sendeth the springs into the valleys,
And his breath is in the mighty trees.
In his hand are the deep places of the earth:
The strength of the hills is his also.
The sea is his,
And his hands formed the dry land.
All the heavens declare the Glory of God,
And the firmament showeth his Law.
And to his children
Doth he bequeath his Kingdom,
To those who walk with his Angels,
And find their peace with his Holy Law.

Wouldst thou know more, my children?
How may we speak with our lips
That which cannot be spoken?
It is like a pomegranate eaten by a mute:
How then may he tell of its flavor?
If we say the Heavenly Father
Dwelleth within us,
Then are the heavens ashamed;
If we say he dwelleth without us,
It is falsehood.
The eye which scanneth the far horizon
And the eye which seeth the hearts of men
He maketh as one eye.
He is not manifest,
He is not hidden.
He is not revealed,
Nor is he unrevealed.
My children, there are no words
To tell that which he is!
Only this do we know:
We are his children,
And he is our Father.
He is our God,
And we are the children of his pasture,
And the sheep of his hand.
He who hath found peace
With his Heavenly Father
Hath entered the Sanctuary
Of the Holy Law,
And hath made a covenant with God
Which shall endure forever.
Know this peace with thy mind,

Desire this peace with thy heart,
Fulfill this peace with thy body.
Though heaven and earth may pass away,
Not one letter of the Holy Law
Shall change or pass away.
For in the beginning was the Law,
And the Law was with God,
And the Law was God.
May the Sevenfold Peace
Of the Heavenly Father
Be with thee always.

FRAGMENTS IDENTICAL WITH THE DEAD SEA SCROLLS

And Enoch walked with God;
and he was not;
for God took him.

Essene Genesis 5:24

The Law was planted in the garden of the
    Brotherhood
to enlighten the heart of man
and to make straight before him
all the ways of true righteousness,
an humble spirit, an even temper,
a freely compassionate nature,
and eternal goodness and understanding and insight,
and mighty wisdom which believes in all God's
    works
and a confident trust in His many blessings
and a spirit of knowledge in all things of the Great
    Order,
loyal feelings toward all the children of truth,
a radiant purity which loathes everything impure,
a discretion regarding all the hidden things of truth
and secrets of inner knowledge.

from the Manual of Discipline
of the Dead Sea Scrolls

Thou hast made known unto me
Thy deep, mysterious things.
All things exist by Thee
and there is none beside Thee.
By Thy Law

Thou hast directed my heart
that I set my steps straight forward
upon right paths
and walk where Thy presence is.

from the Book of Hymns VII
of the Dead Sea Scrolls

The Law was planted to reward the children of light
with healing and abundant peace,
with long life,
with fruitful seed of everlasting blessings,
with eternal joy
in immortality of eternal Light.

from the Manual of Discipline
of the Dead Sea Scrolls

I thank Thee, Heavenly Father,
because Thou hast put me
at a source of running streams,
at a living spring in a land of drought,
watering an eternal garden of wonders,
the Tree of Life, mystery of mysteries,
growing everlasting branches for eternal planting
to sink their roots into the stream of life
from an eternal source.
And Thou, Heavenly Father,
protect their fruits
with the angels of the day
and of the night
and with flames of eternal Light burning every way.

from the Thanksgiving Psalms
of the Dead Sea Scrolls

I am grateful, Heavenly Father,
for Thou hast raised me to an eternal height
and I walk in the wonders of the plain.
Thou gavest me guidance
to reach Thine eternal company
from the depths of the earth.
Thou hast purified my body
to join the army of the angels of the earth
and my spirit to reach
the congregation of the heavenly angels.
Thou gavest man eternity
to praise at dawn and dusk
Thy works and wonders
in joyful song.

from the Thanksgiving Psalms
of the Dead Sea Scrolls

I will praise Thy works
with songs of Thanksgiving
continually, from period to period,
in the circuits of the day, and in its fixed order;
with the coming of light from its source
and at the turn of evening and the outgoing of light,
at the outgoing of darkness and the coming in of day,
continually,
in all the generations of time.

from the Thanksgiving Psalms
of the Dead Sea Scrolls

May He bless thee with every good,
may He keep thee from all evil
and illumine thy heart with the knowledge of life

and favor thee with eternal wisdom.
And may He give His Sevenfold blessings upon thee
to everlasting Peace.

from the Manual of Discipline
of the Dead Sea Scrolls

With the coming of day
I embrace my Mother,
with the coming of night
I join my Father,
and with the outgoing of evening and morning
I will breathe Their Law,
and I will not interrupt these Communions
until the end of time.

from the Manual of Discipline
of the Dead Sea Scrolls

He assigned to man two spirits with which he
        should walk.
They are the spirits of truth and of falsehood,
truth born out of the spring of Light,
falsehood from the well of darkness.
The dominion of all the children of truth
is in the hands of the Angels of Light
so that they walk in the ways of Light.
The spirits of truth and falsehood struggle within
        the heart of man,
behaving with wisdom and folly.
And according as a man inherits truth
so will he avoid darkness.
Blessings on all that have cast their lot with the Law,
that walk truthfully in all their ways.

May the Law bless them with all good
and keep them from all evil
and illumine their hearts with insight into the things
  of life
and grace them with knowledge of things eternal.

from the Manual of Discipline
of the Dead Sea Scrolls

I have reached the inner vision
and through Thy spirit in me
I have heard Thy wondrous secret.
Through Thy mystic insight
Thou hast caused a spring of knowledge
to well up within me,
a fountain of power,
pouring forth living waters,
a flood of love
and of all-embracing wisdom
like the splendor of eternal Light.

from the Book of Hymns of the Dead Sea Scrolls

FROM THE ESSENE BOOK
OF
THE TEACHER OF RIGHTEOUSNESS

And the Master took himself to the banks of a stream where the people were gathered, those who did hunger after his words. And he blessed them, and asked them whereof they were troubled. And one did speak: "Master, tell us what are those things we should hold of high value, and what are those things we should despise?"

And the Master answered, saying, "All the ills which men suffer are caused by those things without us; for what is within us can never make us suffer. A child dies, a fortune is lost, house and fields burn, and all men are helpless, and they cry out, 'What shall I do now? What shall now befall me? Will this thing come to pass?' All these are the words of those who grieve and rejoice over events which do befall them, events which are not of their doing. But if we do mourn over that which is not in our power, we are as the little child who weeps when the sun leaves the sky. It was said of old, thou shalt not covet any thing that is thy neighbor's; and now I say unto thee, thou shalt not desire any thing which is not in thy power, for only that which is within thee doth belong to thee; and that which is without thee doth belong to another. In this doth happiness lie: to know what is thine, and what is not thine. If thou wouldst have eternal life, hold fast to the eternity within thee, and grasp not at the shadows of the world of men, which hold the seeds of death."

"Is not all that happens without thee, outside of thy power? It is. And thy knowledge of good and evil, is it not within thee? It is. Is it not, then, in thy power, to treat of all which doth come to pass in the light of wisdom and love, instead of sadness and despair? It is. Can any man hinder thee from doing thus? No man can. Then shalt thou not cry out, 'What shall I do? What shall now befall me? Will this thing come to pass?' For whatsoever may come to pass, thou shalt judge it in the light of wisdom and love, and see all things with the eyes of the Angels."

"For to weigh thy happiness according to that which may befall thee, is to live as a slave. And to live according to the Angels which speak within thee, is to be free. Thou shalt live in freedom as a true son of God, and bow thy head only to the commandments of the Holy Law. In this way shalt thou live, that when the Angel of Death cometh for thee, thou canst stretch out thy hands to God, and say, 'The Communions I have received from thee for knowing thy Law and walking in the paths of the Angels, I have not neglected: I have not dishonored thee by my acts: see how I have used the eye which seeth within: have I ever blamed thee? Have I cried out against that which hath befallen me, or desired that it be otherwise? Have I desired to transgress thy Law? That thou hast given me life, I thank thee for what thou hast given me: so long as I have used the things which are thine, I am content: take them back and place them wherever thou mayest choose, for thine are all things, even unto eternity.' "

"Know ye, that no man can serve two masters. Thou canst not wish to have the world's riches, and have also the Kingdom of Heaven. Thou canst not wish to own lands and wield power over men, and have also the Kingdom of Heaven. Wealth, lands and power, these things belong to no man, for they are of the world. But the Kingdom of Heaven is thine forever, for it is within thee. And if thou dost desire and seek after that which doth not belong to thee, then shalt thou surely lose that which is thine. Know ye, for I tell thee truly, that nothing is given nor is it had for nothing. For every thing in the world of men and angels, there is a price. He who would gather wealth and riches must run about, kiss the hands of those he admires not, waste himself with fatigue at other men's doors, say and do many false things, give gifts of gold and silver and sweet oils; all this and more must a man do to gather wealth and favor. And when thou hast achieved it, what then dost thou have? Will this wealth and power secure for thee freedom from fear, a mind at peace, a day spent in the company of the Angels of the Earthly Mother, a night spent in communion with the Angels of the Heavenly Father? Dost thou expect to have for nothing, things so great? When a man hath two masters, either he will hate the one, and love the other; or else he will hold to the one, and despise the other. Ye cannot serve God and also serve the world. Perchance thy well goeth dry, precious oil is spilled, thy house burneth, thy crops wither: but thou dost treat what may befall thee with wisdom and love. Rains again shall fill the well, houses can again be built, new seeds can be sown: all these things shall pass away, and come again, and yet again pass away. But the kingdom of heaven is eternal, and shall not pass away. Do ye not, then, barter that which is eternal, for that which dieth in an hour."

* * *

When men shall ask of thee, to what country dost thou belong, say ye not that thou art of this country or that, for of truth, it is only the poor body which is born in one small corner of this earth. But thou, O Child of Light, belongeth to the Brotherhood which doth encompass all the heavens and beyond, and from thy Heavenly Father hath descended the seeds not only of thy father and grandfather, but of all beings which are generated on the earth. In truth, thou art a son of God, and all men thy brothers: and to have God for thy maker and thy father and guardian, shall not this release us from all sorrow and fear?

Therefore, I say unto thee, take no thought to store up worldly goods, possessions, gold and silver, for these bring only corruption and death. For the greater thy hoard of wealth, the thicker shall be the walls of thy tomb. Open wide the windows of thy soul, and breathe the fresh air of a free man! Why take ye thought for raiment? Consider the lilies of the field, how they grow: they toil not, neither do they spin: and yet I say unto thee, that even Solomon in his glory was not arrayed like one of these. Why take ye thought for nourishment? Consider the gifts of thy Earthly Mother: the ripe fruits of her trees, and the golden grain of her soil. Why take ye thought for house and lands? A man cannot sell to thee that which he doth not own, and he cannot own that which already doth belong to all. This wide earth is thine, and all men are thy brothers. The Angels of the Earthly Mother walk with thee by day, and the Angels of the Heavenly Father guide thee by night, and within thee is the Holy Law. It is not meet for the son of a king to covet a bauble in the gutter. Take thy place, then, at the table of the celebration, and fulfill thy inheritance with honor. For in God we live, and move, and have our being. In truth, we are his sons, and he is our Father.

* * *

He only is free who liveth as he doth desire to live; who is not hindered in his acts, and whose desires attaineth their ends. He who is not restrained is free, but he who can be restrained or hindered, that man is surely a slave. But who is not a slave? That man only who desireth nothing which doth belong to others. And what are those things which belong to thee? My children, only the kingdom of heaven within thee, where the Law of thy Heavenly Father doth dwell, doth belong to thee. The kingdom of heaven is like unto a merchant man, seeking goodly pearls: who, when he had found one pearl of great price, went and sold all that he had, and bought it. And if this one precious pearl be thine forever, why dost thou barter it for pebbles and stones? Know ye, that thy house, thy land, thy sons and daughters, all the joys of fortune and sorrows of tribulation, yea, even that opinion which others do hold of thee, all these things belong to thee not. And if ye then do lust after these things, and hold fast to them, and grieve and exult over them, then in truth thou art a slave, and in slavery wilt thou remain.

My children, let not the things which are not thine cleave unto thee! Let not the world grow unto thee, as the creeping vine groweth fast to the oak, so that thou dost suffer pain when it is torn from thee. Naked camest thou from thy mother's womb, and naked shalt thou return thither. The world giveth and the world taketh away. But no power in heaven or earth can take from thee the Holy Law which doth reside within thee. Thou mayest see thy parents slain, and from thy country mayest thou be driven. Then shalt thou go with cheerful heart to live in another, and look with pity on the slayer of thy parents, knowing that by the deed he doth slay himself. For thou knowest thy true parents, and thou livest secure in thy true country. For thy true parents are thy Heavenly Father and thy Earthly Mother, and thy true country is the Kingdom of Heaven. Death can never separate thee from thy true parents, and from thy true country there is no exile. And within thee, a rock which standeth against all storms, is the Holy Law, thy bulwark and thy salvation.

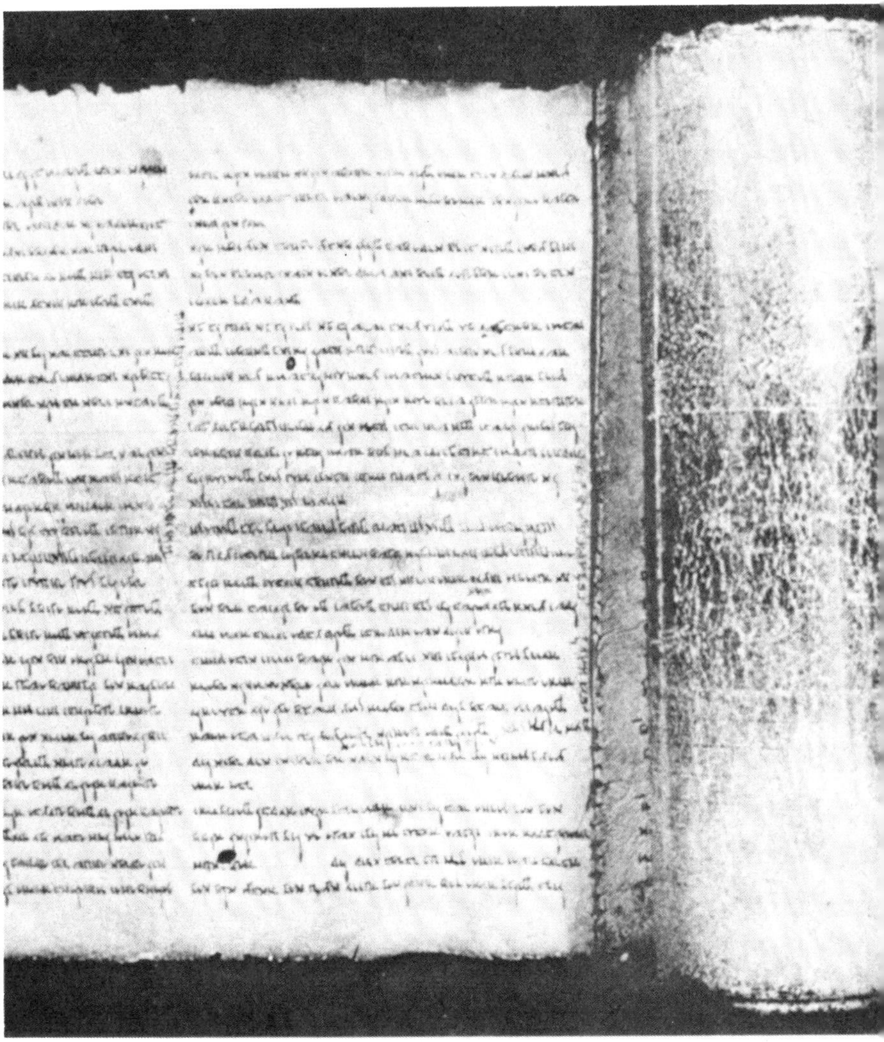

FRAGMENTS FROM THE ESSENE GOSPEL OF JOHN

In the beginning was the Law, and the Law was with God, and the Law was God. The same was in the beginning with God. All things were made by him; and without him was not anything made that was made. In him was life; and the life was the light of men. And the light shineth in the darkness; and the darkness comprehended it not.

From the far place in the desert came the Brothers, to bear witness of the Light, that all men through them might walk in the light of the Holy Law. For the true light doth illumine every man that cometh into the world, but the world knoweth it not. But as many do receive the Law, to them is given the power to become the Sons of God, and to enter the Eternal Sea where standeth the Tree of Life.

And Jesus taught them, saying, Verily, verily, I say unto thee, except a man be born again, he cannot see the Kingdom of Heaven.

And one man said, How can a man be born when he is old? Can he enter a second time into his mother's womb, and be born?

And Jesus answered, Verily, verily, I say unto thee, Except a man be born of the Earthly Mother and the Heavenly Father, and walk with the Angels of the Day and the Night, he cannot enter into the Eternal Kingdom. That which is born of the flesh is flesh; and that which is born of the Spirit is spirit. And the flesh of thy body is born of the Earthly Mother, and the spirit within thee is born of the Heavenly Father. The wind bloweth where it listeth, and thou hearest the sound thereof, but canst not tell whence it cometh. So it is with the Holy Law. All men hear it, but know it not, for from their first breath it is with them. But he who is born again of the Heavenly Father and the Earthly Mother, he shall hear with new ears, and see with new eyes, and the flame of the Holy Law shall be kindled within him.

And one man asked, How can these things be?

Jesus answered and said unto him, Verily, verily, I say unto thee, We speak that we do know, and testify that we have seen;

and ye receive not our witness. For man is born to walk with the Angels, but instead he doth search for jewels in the mud. To him hath the Heavenly Father bestowed his inheritance, that he should build the Kingdom of Heaven on earth, but man hath turned his back on his Father, and doth worship the world and its idols. And this is the condemnation, that light is come into the world, and men loved darkness rather than light, because their deeds were evil. For every one that doeth evil hateth the light, neither cometh to the light. For we are all Sons of God, and in us God is glorified. And the light which shineth around God and his children is the Light of the Holy Law. And he who hateth the light, doth deny his Father and his Mother, who have given him birth.

And one man asked, Master, how can we know the light?

And Jesus answered, Verily, verily, I give unto thee a new commandment: that ye love one another, even as they love thee who work together in the Garden of the Brotherhood. By this shall all men know that ye too are brothers, even as we all are Sons of God.

And one man said, All thy talk is of the brotherhood, yet we cannot all be of the brotherhood. Yet we would worship light and shun darkness, for none there is among us who desireth evil.

And Jesus answered, Let not thy heart be troubled: ye believe in God. Know ye that in our Father's house are many mansions, and our brotherhood is but a dark glass reflecting the Heavenly Brotherhood unto which all creatures of heaven and earth do belong. The brotherhood is the vine, and our Heavenly Father is the husbandman. Every branch in us that beareth not fruit he taketh away: and every branch that beareth fruit, he purgeth it, that it may bring forth more fruit. Abide in us, and we in thee. As the branch cannot bear fruit of itself, except it abide in the vine, no more can ye, except ye abide in the Holy Law, which is the rock upon which our brotherhood stands. He that abideth in the Law, the same bringeth forth much fruit: for without the Law ye can do nothing. If a man abide not in the Law, he is cast forth as a branch, and is withered; and men gather them, and cast them into the fire, and they are burned.

And as the brothers abide in the love one for another, as the Angel of Love doth teach them, so we do ask that ye love one another. Greater love hath no man than this, to teach the Holy Law one to another, and to love each other as oneself. The Heavenly Father is in us, and we are in him, and we do reach out our hands in love and ask that ye be one in us. The glory which he gavest us we do give to thee: that thou mayest be one, even as we are one. For thy Father in Heaven hath loved thee before the foundation of the world.

And in this manner did the Brothers teach the Holy Law to them who would hear it, and it is said they did marvelous things, and healed the sick and afflicted with diverse grasses and wondrous uses of sun and water. And there are also many other things they did, the which, if they should be written every one, even the world itself could not contain the books that should be written. Amen.

FRAGMENTS FROM

THE ESSENE BOOK OF REVELATIONS

Behold, the Angel of Air shall bring him,
And every eye shall see him,
And the brotherhood,
All the vast brotherhood of the earth
Shall raise their voice as one and sing,
Because of him.
Even so, Amen.

I am Alpha and Omega, the beginning and the end;
Which is, which was, and which is to come.

And the voice spoke, and I turned to see
The voice that spoke with me.
And being turned, I saw seven golden candles;
And in the midst of their blazing light
I saw one like unto the Son of Man,
Clothed in white, white as the snow.
And his voice filled the air with the sound of rushing water;
And in his hands were seven stars,
Full of the flaming light of the heavens from whence they came.
And when he spoke, his face was streaming light,
Blazing and golden like a thousand suns.

And he said, "Fear not, I am the first and the last;
I am the beginning and the end.
Write the things which thou hast seen,
And the things which are, and the things which shall be hereafter;
The mystery of the seven stars which fill my hands,
And the seven golden candles, blazing with eternal light.
The seven stars are the Angels of the Heavenly Father,
And the seven candles are the Angels of the Earthly Mother.

And the spirit of man is the flame
Which streams between the starlight and the glowing candle:
A bridge of holy light between heaven and earth.

These things saith he that holdeth seven stars in his hands,
Who walketh in the midst of the flames of seven golden candles.
He that hath an ear, let him hear what the Spirit saith:
"To him that overcometh will I give to eat of the Tree of Life,
That standeth in the midst of the shining Paradise of God."

And then I looked, and, behold,
A door was opened in heaven:
And a voice which sounded from all sides, like a trumpet,
Spoke to me: "Come up hither,
And I will show thee things which must be hereafter."

And immediately I was there, in spirit,
At the threshold of the open door.
And I entered through the open door
Into a sea of blazing light.
And in the midst of the blinding ocean of radiance was a throne;
And on the throne sat one whose face was hidden.
And there was a rainbow round about the throne,
In sight like unto an emerald.
And round about the throne were thirteen seats:
And upon the seats I saw thirteen elders sitting,
Clothed in white raiment;
And their faces were hidden by swirling clouds of light.
And seven lamps of fire burned before the throne,
The fire of the Earthly Mother.
And seven stars of heaven shone before the throne,
The fire of the Heavenly Father.
And before the throne
There was a sea of glass like unto crystal:

And reflected therein
Were all the mountains and valleys and oceans of the earth,
And all the creatures abiding therein.
And the thirteen elders bowed down before the splendor of him
Who sat on the throne, whose face was hidden,
And rivers of light streamed from their hands, one to the other,
And they cried, "Holy, holy, holy,
Lord God Almighty,
Which was, and is, and is to come.
Thou art worthy, O Lord,
To receive glory and honor and power:
For thou hast created all things."

And then I saw in the right hand
Of him that sat on the throne,
Whose face was hidden,
A book written within and on the backside,
Sealed with seven seals.
And I saw an angel proclaiming with a loud voice,
"Who is worthy to open the book,
And to loose the seals thereof?"

And no being in heaven, nor in earth, neither under the earth,
Was able to open the book, neither to look thereon.
And I wept, because the book could not be opened,
Nor was I able to read what there was written.
And one of the elders saith unto me, "Weep not.
Reach out thy hand, and take the book,
Yea, even the book with the seven seals, and open it.
For it was written for thee,
Who art at once the lowest of the low,
And the highest of the high."

And I reached out my hand and touched the book.

And, behold, the cover lifted,
And my hands touched the golden pages,
And my eyes beheld the mystery of the seven seals.

And I beheld, and I heard the voice of many angels
Round about the throne,
And the number of them was ten thousand times ten thousand,
And thousands of thousands, saying with a loud voice,
"All glory, and wisdom, and strength,
And power forever and ever,
To him who shall reveal the Mystery of Mysteries."
And I saw the swirling clouds of golden light
Stretching like a fiery bridge between my hands,
And the hands of the thirteen elders,
And the feet of him who sat on the throne,
Whose face was hidden.

And I opened the first seal.
And I saw, and beheld the Angel of Air.
And between her lips flowed the breath of life,
And she knelt over the earth
And gave to man the winds of Wisdom.
And man breathed in.
And when he breathed out, the sky darkened,
And the sweet air became foul and fetid,
And clouds of evil smoke hung low over all the earth.
And I turned my face away in shame.

And I opened the second seal.
And I saw, and beheld the Angel of Water.
And between her lips flowed the water of life,
And she knelt over the earth
And gave to man an ocean of Love.
And man entered the clear and shining waters.

And when he touched the water, the clear streams darkened,
And the crystal waters became thick with slime,
And the fish lay gasping in the foul blackness,
And all creatures died of thirst.
And I turned my face away in shame.

And I opened the third seal.
And I saw, and beheld the Angel of Sun.
And between her lips flowed the light of life,
And she knelt over the earth
And gave to man the fires of Power.
And the strength of the sun entered the heart of man,
And he took the power, and made with it a false sun,
And, lo, he spread the fires of destruction,
Burning the forests, laying waste the green valleys,
Leaving only charred bones of his brothers.
And I turned my face away in shame.

And I opened the fourth seal.
And I saw, and beheld the Angel of Joy.
And between her lips flowed the music of life,
And she knelt over the earth
And gave to man the song of Peace.
And peace and joy like music
Flowed through the soul of man.
But he heard only the harsh discord of sadness and discontent,
And he lifted up his sword
And cut off the hands of the peacemakers,
And lifted it up once again
And cut off the heads of the singers.
And I turned my face away in shame.

And I opened the fifth seal.
And I saw, and beheld the Angel of Life.

And between her lips
Flowed the holy alliance between God and Man,
And she knelt over the earth
And gave to man the gift of Creation.
And man created a sickle of iron in the shape of a serpent,
And the harvest he reaped was hunger and death.
And I turned my face away in shame.

And I opened the sixth seal.
And I saw, and beheld the Angel of Earth.
And between her lips flowed the river of Eternal Life,
And she knelt over the earth
And gave to man the secret of eternity,
And told him to open his eyes
And behold the mysterious Tree of Life in the Endless Sea.
But man lifted his hand and put out his own eyes,
And said there was no eternity.
And I turned my face away in shame.

And I opened the seventh seal.
And I saw, and beheld the Angel of the Earthly Mother.
And she brought with her a message of blazing light
From the throne of the Heavenly Father.
And this message was for the ears of man alone,
He who walks between earth and heaven.
And into the ear of man was whispered the message.
And he did not hear.
But I did not turn away my face in shame.
Lo, I reached forth my hand to the wings of the angel,
And I turned my voice to heaven, saying,
"Tell me the message. For I would eat of the fruit
Of the Tree of Life that grows in the Sea of Eternity."
And the angel looked upon me with great sadness,

And there was silence in heaven.
And then I heard a voice, which was like unto the voice
Which sounded like a trumpet, saying,
"O Man, wouldst thou look upon the evil thou hast wrought,
When thou didst turn thy face away from the throne of God,
When thou didst not make use of the gifts
Of the seven Angels of the Earthly Mother
And the seven Angels of the Heavenly Father?
And a terrible pain seized me as I felt within me
The souls of all those who had blinded themselves,
So as to see only their own desires of the flesh.
And I saw the seven angels which stood before God;
And to them were given seven trumpets.
And another angel came and stood at the altar,
Having a golden censer;
And there was given unto him much incense,
That he should offer it with the prayers of all the angels
Upon the golden altar which was before the throne.
And the smoke of the incense ascended up before God
Out of the angel's hand.
And the angel took the censer,
And filled it with the fire of the altar,
And cast it into the earth,
And there were voices and thunderings,
And lightnings, and earthquakes.
And the seven angels which had the seven trumpets
Prepared themselves to sound.

The first angel sounded,
And there followed hail and fire mingled with blood,
And they were cast upon the earth:
And the green forests and trees were burnt up,
And all green grass shriveled to cinders.

And the second angel sounded,
And as it were a great mountain burning with fire
Was cast into the sea:
And blood rose from the earth as a vapor.

And the third angel sounded,
And lo, there was a great earthquake;
And the sun became as black as sackcloth of hair,
And the moon became as blood.

And the fourth angel sounded,
And the stars of heaven fell onto the earth,
Even as a fig tree casteth her untimely figs,
When she is shaken of a mighty wind.

And the fifth angel sounded,
And the heaven departed as a scroll when it is rolled together.
And over the whole earth there was not one tree,
Nor one flower, nor one blade of grass.
And I stood on the earth,
And my feet sank into the soil, soft and thick with blood,
Stretching as far as the eye could see.
And over all the earth was silence.

And the sixth angel sounded.
And I saw a mighty being come down from heaven,
Clothed with a cloud:
And a rainbow was upon his head,
And his face was as it were the sun,
And his feet were pillars of fire.
And he had in his hand an open book:
And he set his right foot upon the sea, and his left on the earth,
And he cried with a loud voice, which was wondrous to hear:
"O Man, wouldst thou have this vision come to pass?"

And I answered, "Thou knowest, O Holy One,
That I would do anything
That these terrible things might not come to pass."

And he spoke: "Man has created these powers of destruction.
He has wrought them from his own mind.
He has turned his face away
From the Angels of the Heavenly Father and the Earthly Mother,
And he has fashioned his own destruction."

And I spoke: "Then is there no hope, bright angel?"
And a blazing light streamed like a river from his hands
As he answered, "There is always hope,
O thou for whom heaven and earth were created."

And then the angel,
He who stood upon the sea and upon the earth,
Lifted up his hand to heaven,
And swore by him that liveth for ever and ever,
Who created heaven, and the things that therein are,
And the earth, and the things that therein are,
And the sea, and the things which are therein,
That there should be time no longer:
But in the days of the voice of the seventh angel,
When he shall begin to sound,
The mystery of God should be revealed to those
Who have eaten from the Tree of Life

Which standeth for ever in the Eternal Sea.
And the voice spoke again, saying:
"Go, and take the book which is open in the hand of the angel
Which standeth upon the sea and upon the earth."
And I went unto the angel, and said unto him,
"Give me the book,
For I would eat from the Tree of Life

Which standeth in the middle of the Eternal Sea."
And the angel gave to me the book,
And I opened the book, and I read therein
What had always been, what was now,
And what would come to pass.

I saw the holocaust which would engulf the earth,
And the great destruction
Which would drown all her people in oceans of blood.
And I saw too the eternity of man
And the endless forgiveness of the Almighty.
The souls of men were as blank pages in the book,
Always ready for a new song to be there inscribed.

And I lifted up my face
To the seven Angels of the Earthly Mother
And the seven Angels of the Heavenly Father,
And I felt my feet touching the holy brow of the Earthly Mother,
And my fingers touching the holy feet of the Heavenly Father,
And I uttered a hymn of Thanksgiving:

> I thank thee, Heavenly Father,
> Because thou hast put me at a source of running streams,
> At a living spring in a land of drought,
> Watering an eternal garden of wonders,
> The Tree of Life, Mystery of Mysteries,
> Growing everlasting branches for eternal planting
> To sink their roots into the stream of life
> From an eternal source.
> And thou, Heavenly Father,
> Protect their fruits
> With the Angels of the day and of the night
> And with flames of Eternal Light burning every way.

But again the voice spoke,

And again my eyes were drawn away
From the splendors of the realm of light.
"Heed thou, O Man!
Thou mayest step on the right path
And walk in the presence of the Angels.
Thou mayest sing of the Earthly Mother by day
And of the Heavenly Father by night,
And through thy being may course the golden stream of the Law.
But wouldst thou leave thy brothers
To plunge through the gaping chasm of blood,
As the pain-wracked earth shudders and groans
Under her chains of stone?
Canst thou drink of the cup of eternal life,
When thy brothers die of thirst?

And my heart was heavy with compassion,
And I looked, and lo,
There appeared a great wonder in heaven:
A woman clothed with the sun, and the moon under her feet,
And upon her head a crown of seven stars.
And I knew she was the source of running streams
And the Mother of the Forests.

And I stood upon the sand of the sea,
And saw a beast rise up out of the sea,
And from his nostrils wafted foul and loathsome air,
And where he rose from the sea the clear waters turned to slime,
And his body was covered with black and steaming stone.
And the woman clothed with the sun
Reached out her arms to the beast,
And the beast drew near and embraced her.
And lo, her skin of pearl withered beneath his foul breath,
And her back was broken by his arms of crushing rock,

And with tears of blood she sank into the pool of slime.
And from the mouth of the beast there poured armies of men,
Brandishing swords and fighting, one with the other.
And they fought with a terrible anger,
And they cut off their own limbs and clawed out their eyes,
Until they fell into the pit of slime,
Screaming in agony and pain.

And I stepped to the edge of the pool and reached down my hand,
And I could see the swirling maelstrom of blood,
And the men therein, trapped like flies in a web.
And I spoke in a loud voice, saying,
"Brothers, drop thy swords and take hold of my hand.
Leave off this defiling and desecration of she
Who hath given thee birth,
And he who hath given thee thy inheritance.
For thy days of buying and selling are over,
And over, too, thy days of hunting and killing.
For he that leadeth into captivity shall go into captivity,
And he that killeth by the sword must be killed with the sword.
And the merchants of the earth shall weep and mourn,
For no man buyeth thy merchandise any more:
The merchants of gold, and silver, and precious stones,
And of pearls, and fine linen, and purple, and silk, and scarlet,
And marble and beasts, and sheep and horses,
And chariots and slaves and souls of men,
All these things can ye not buy and sell,
For all is buried in a sea of blood
Because thou hast turned thy back on thy father and mother,
And worshipped the beast who would build a paradise of stone.
Drop thy swords, my brothers, and take hold of my hand.

And as our fingers clasped,

I saw in the distance a great city,
White and shining on the far horizon, glowing alabaster.
And there were voices, and thunders, and lightnings,
And there was a great earthquake,
Such as was not since men were upon the earth,
So mighty an earthquake, and so great.
And the great city was divided into three parts,
And the cities of the nations fell:
And the great city came in remembrance before God,
To give unto her the cup of the wine
Of the fierceness of his wrath.
And every island fled away, and the mountains were not found.
And there fell upon men a great hail out of heaven,
Every stone about the weight of a talent.
And a mighty angel took up a stone like a great millstone,
And cast it into the sea, saying,
"Thus with violence shall the great city be thrown down,
And shall be found no more at all.
And the voice of harpers, and musicians, and of pipers,
And of singers, and trumpeters,
Shall be heard no more at all in thee;
And no craftsman, of whatsoever craft he be,
Shall be found any more in thee;
And the sound of a millstone shall be heard
No more at all in thee.
And the light of a candle shall shine
No more at all in thee;·
And the voice of the bridegroom and of the bride shall be heard
No more at all in thee:
For thy merchants were the great men of the earth;
For by thy sorceries were all nations deceived.
And in her was found the blood of prophets, and of saints,

And of all that were slain upon the earth."

And my brothers laid hold of my hand,
And they struggled out of the pool of slime
And stood bewildered on the sea of sand,
And skies opened and washed their naked bodies with rain.
And I heard a voice from heaven, as the voice of many waters,
And as the voice of a great thunder:
And I heard the voice of harpers harping with their harps.
And they sung as it were a new song before the throne.

And I saw another angel fly in the midst of heaven,
Having the songs of day and night
And the everlasting gospel to preach unto them
That dwell on the earth,
Unto them that have climbed from the pit of slime
And stand naked and washed by the rain before the throne.
And the angel cried, "Fear God, and give glory to him;
For the hour of his judgment is come:
And worship him that made heaven, and earth,
And the sea, and the fountains of waters."

And I saw heaven open, and beheld a white horse;
And he that sat upon him was called Faithful and True,
And in Righteousness he doth judge.
His eyes were as a flame of fire,
And on his head were many crowns,
And he was cloaked in blazing light
And his feet were bare.
And his name is called the Word of God.
And the Holy Brotherhood followed him upon white horses,
Clothed in fine linen, white and clean.
And they entered the eternal Infinite Garden,
In whose midst stood the Tree of Life.

And the rain-washed naked throngs came before them,
Trembling to receive their judgment.
For their sins were many, and they had defiled the earth,
Yea, they had destroyed the creatures of the land and sea,
Poisoned the ground, fouled the air,
And buried alive the Mother who had given them birth.

But I saw not what befell them, for my vision changed,
And I saw a new heaven and a new earth:
For the first heaven and the first earth were passed away;
And there was no more sea.
And I saw the holy city of the Brotherhood
Coming down from God out of heaven,
Prepared as a bride adorned for her husband.
And I heard a great voice out of heaven saying,
"Lo, the mountain of the Lord's house
Is established in the top of the mountains
And is exalted above the hills;
And all people shall flow unto it.
Come ye, and let us go up to the mountain of the Lord,
To the house of God;
And he will teach us of his ways,
And we will walk in his paths:
For out of the Holy Brotherhood shall go forth the Law.
Behold, the tabernacle of God is with men,
And he will dwell with them, and they shall be his people,
And God himself shall be with them, and be their God.
And God shall wipe away all tears from their eyes;
And there shall be no more death,
Neither sorrow, nor crying,
Neither shall there be any more pain:
For the former things are passed away.

Those who made war shall beat their swords into plowshares,
And their spears into pruninghooks:
Nation shall not lift up sword against nation,
Neither shall they learn war any more:
For the former things are passed away."

And he spoke again: "Behold, I make all things new.
I am Alpha and Omega, the beginning and the end.
I will give unto him that is athirst
Of the fountain of the water of life freely.
He that overcometh shall inherit all things,
And I will be his God, and he shall be my son.
But the fearful, and unbelieving,
And the abominable, and murderers, and all liars,
Shall dig their own pit which burneth with fire and brimstone."

And again my vision changed,
And I heard the voices of the Holy Brotherhood raised in song,
Saying, "Come ye, and let us walk in the light of the Law."
And I saw the holy city,
And the Brothers were streaming unto it.
And the city had no need of the sun,
Neither of the moon, to shine in it:
For the glory of God did lighten it.
And I saw the pure river of the Water of Life,
Clear as crystal, proceeding out of the throne of God.
And in the midst of the river stood the Tree of Life,
Which bore fourteen manner of fruits,
And yielded her fruit to those who would eat of it,
And the leaves of the tree were for the healing of the nations.
And there shall be no night there;
And they need no candle, neither light of the sun,
For the Lord God giveth them light:

And they shall reign for ever and ever.

> *I have reached the inner vision*
> *And through thy spirit in me*
> *I have heard thy wondrous secret.*
> *Through thy mystic insight*
> *Thou hast caused a spring of knowledge*
> *To well up within me,*
> *A fountain of power, pouring forth living waters;*
> *A flood of love and of all-embracing wisdom*
> *Like the splendor of Eternal Light.*

THE STORY OF THE ESSENE GOSPEL OF PEACE

Translated by Edmond Bordeaux Szekely

In Four Volumes

It was in 1928 that Edmond Bordeaux Szekely first published his translation of Book One of *The Essene Gospel of Peace*, an ancient manuscript he had found in the Secret Archives of the Vatican as the result of limitless patience, faultless scholarship, and unerring intuition. This story is told in his book *The Discovery of the Essene Gospel of Peace*, published in 1975. The English version of Book One appeared in 1937, and ever since, the little volume has traveled over the world, appearing in many different languages, gaining every year more and more readers, until now, still with no commercial advertisement, over a million copies have been sold in the United States alone. It was not until almost fifty years after the first French translation that Book Two and Book Three appeared *(The Unknown Books of the Essenes* and *Lost Scrolls of the Essene Brotherhood)*, achieving rapidly the popularity of Book One.

In 1981, Book Four, *The Teachings of the Elect*, was published posthumously according to Dr. Szekely's wishes, representing yet another fragment of the complete manuscript which exists in Aramaic in the Secret Archives of the Vatican and in old Slavonic in the Royal Library of the Habsburgs in Austria. The poetic style of the translator brings to vivid reality the exquisitely beautiful words of Jesus and the Elders of the Essene Brotherhood. Some of the chapters: The Essene Communions. The Sevenfold Peace. The Holy Streams of Life, Light, and Sound. The Gift of the Humble Grass.

All four volumes of *The Essene Gospel of Peace* are available in English from the International Biogenic Society, mailing address: I.B.S. Internacional, P.O. Box 849, Nelson, B.C., Canada V1L 6A5. A free descriptive catalogue of these and all the collected works of Edmond Bordeaux Szekely will be gladly sent upon request.

CREDO

of the International Biogenic Society

We believe that our most precious possession is Life.

We believe we shall mobilize all the forces of Life against the forces of death.

We believe that mutual understanding leads toward mutual cooperation; that mutual cooperation leads toward Peace; and that Peace is the only way of survival for mankind.

We believe that we shall preserve instead of waste our natural resources, which are the heritage of our children.

We believe that we shall avoid the pollution of our air, water, and soil, the basic preconditions of Life.

We believe we shall preserve the vegetation of our planet: the humble grass which came fifty million years ago, and the majestic trees which came twenty million years ago, to prepare our planet for mankind.

We believe we shall eat only fresh, natural, pure, whole foods, without chemicals and artificial processing.

We believe we shall live a simple, natural, creative life, absorbing all the sources of energy, harmony and knowledge, in and around us.

We believe that the improvement of life and mankind on our planet must start with individual efforts, as the whole depends on the atoms composing it.

We believe in the Fatherhood of God, the Motherhood of Nature, and the Brotherhood of Man.

☐ I feel an affinity with your Credo. Please mail to me your free complete descriptive catalogue of all the books of Dr. Edmond Bordeaux Szekely.

☐ I want to study the complete, all-comprehensive guide and textbook of the International Biogenic Society, *The Essene Way-Biogenic Living.* I enclose my check in U.S. currency of $11.50, plus the minimum postage & handling charge of $3.00.

☐ I want to become an Associate Member of the International Biogenic Society. Membership entitles me to receive free: (1) *The Essene Way-Biogenic Living,* the all-comprehensive guide and I.B.S. textbook; (2) *The Essene Way,* a Periodical Review; (3) 20% discount on all publications of the I.B.S.; and (4) my membership card with all privileges. I enclose my membership fee of U.S. $20.00 (check made out to I.B.S. Internacional, renewable annually.)

Please check the appropriate boxes and return this page to the International Biogenic Society, mailing address: **I.B.S. INTERNACIONAL, P.O. BOX 849, NELSON, BRITISH COLUMBIA, CANADA V1L 6A5.**

*Name*_____

*Address*_____

*City, State/Province, Zip/Code*_____

APPLICATION FOR ASSOCIATE MEMBERSHIP
INTERNATIONAL BIOGENIC SOCIETY

Please return to: *I.B.S. Internacional*
                     P.O. Box 849, Nelson, B.C.
                     Canada V1L 6A5

*Name*_____

*Address*_____

*City, State/Prov.,Zip/Code*_____

*Age*____*Profession*_____

*Previous Experience*_____

I am interested in:

_____*becoming an Associate Member of the I.B.S.*

_____*becoming a Teacher of Biogenic Living.*

Enclosed is my annual Associate Membership fee of U.S.
$20.00. Please mail my membership card, your current
issue of the Periodical Review, *The Essene Way,* and my
copy of *The Essene Way-Biogenic Living,* my "Guidebook,"
textbook, and encyclopedia of ancient wisdom and modern
practice.* I understand I will receive a 20% discount on all
publications as an Associate Member, but only if I order
directly from I.B.S. Internacional.

Please make your check in U.S. currency out to
I.B.S. INTERNACIONAL.

P.S. The only reason we ask
your age, profession and
"previous experience" (what-
ever that means) is just to
get to know you a little, as
we may never have the
chance to meet you per-
sonally. If you don't wish to
answer, it's OK.

*If you already have *The Essene Way-Biogenic Living,* please choose any
other book from our current catalogue for your I.B.S. membership gift.

RECOMMENDED BOOKS FOR STUDY

Many members who have not yet started study groups or live far from book stores and/or like-minded individuals, are interested in a systematic program of home study. The following books are recommended for such a program, and provide an excellent foundation for study of *The Essene Way of Biogenic Living*, especially when coordinated with the methods outlined in *The Art of Study: the Sorbonne Method*.

Please send me the following books:

___*The Essene Gospel of Peace, Book One* $1.00

___*The Essene Gospel of Peace, Book Two* $9.50

___*The Essene Gospel of Peace, Book Three* $9.50

___*The Essene Gospel of Peace, Book Four* $7.50

___*The Essene Way-Biogenic Living* $11.50 *(free with membership)*

___*The Biogenic Revolution* $11.95

___*The Chemistry of Youth* $9.50

___*From Enoch to the Dead Sea Scrolls* $7.50

___*The Essene Book of Creation* $5.95

___*The Essene Code of Life* $4.50

___*The Essene Science of Life* $4.50

___*Essene Communions with the Infinite* $5.95

___*Discovery of the Essene Gospel of Peace* $7.50

___*The Essene Book of Asha* $9.50

___*Books, Our Eternal Companions* $4.50

___*Cosmos, Man and Society* $8.95

___*Search for the Ageless, Volume One* $10.50

___*Search for the Ageless, Volume Two* $11.50

___*The Ecological Health Garden, the Book of Survival* $7.50

___*The Art of Study: the Sorbonne Method* $4.50

_____*Sub-Total*

_____*Add 15% for Postage & Handling ($3.00 minimum)*

U.S. $_____*Total Amount Enclosed*

I.B.S. INTERNACIONAL
Box 849, Nelson, B.C., Canada V1L 6A5

*Name*_____

*Address*_____

*City, State/Province, Zip/Code*_____

All orders must be pre-paid. Minimum order: $10.00, minimum postage: $3.00 (foreign orders may be more). Please make check, bank draft or money order in U.S. FUNDS, drawn on a U.S. BANK, with the proper "microencoding" at the bottom of the check, out to I.B.S. INTERNACIONAL. Allow at least 4 weeks for processing, more for foreign orders. Members and Teachers of the I.B.S. may apply their usual discounts (both must have valid memberships for the current year). *All sales are considered final; please do not return any books.* If there are any questions, PLEASE WRITE before acting, and please print legibly. Dealers and distributors, write for discount information. All books have always been sent from our warehouse in the U.S., hence the necessity for payment in U.S. funds. Thank you! We send you fraternal greetings and hope to hear from you soon!